Seven Cardinal Rules of Debt Avoidance

Femi Adedayo

Seven Cardinal Rules of Debt Avoidance

Published by

Copyright © Global Reach Media

PUBLICATION 2016

Global Reach Media

London, United Kingdom
+447900223577
info@globalreachmedia.co.uk
femiadedayo@yahoo.com
www.globalreachmedia.co.uk

ISBN: 978-0-9932304-3-1

London, United Kingdom

Design By

Other Book by The Author

We set time limits for ourselves, but God is not bound by our time. He made all things and causes all things including time to be. Can we bind Him with the time He created? Absolutely not! This book is written to assure us of God's infallibility.

This book will help us better understand what it meant to wait for God's time. Nothing matters more than allowing God to do what He needs in His appointed time and season.

"Reading this book is plugging into the ocean of spiritual knowledge that will sail you to the shore of a beautiful life"

Pastor Femi Ogunsanya
General Overseer,
Mountain of Transfiguration, Lagos. Nigeria.

"This book shows the deep and loving knowledge and understanding of scripture. Femi has the ability to apply its message to 21st century life"

David Gloin
A local preacher in the Orpinton & Chislehurst Circuit of the British Methodist Church, UK

Contents

Dedication 6

Foreword 7

Preface 9

Rule One: **Learn To Budget** 12

   How To Budget 20

Rule Two : **Learn To Save** 24

   If Ant, You Can 24

   Joseph's Savings Strategy 25

   Coin Jar 30

   Clearance Sales 30

   Do It Yourself 31

   Shop Around 32

   Christmas Club 33

   Tips on how to save 34

Rule Three: **Learn To Pay your Debt** 37

   Prioritize your debts. 39

   'Square peg Debts' 41

   Negotiation 41

   Full and Final Payment 42

   Debt Management Plan 42

   Administration Order 43

   Individual Voluntary Arrangement 43

Debt Relief Order.. 43

Bankruptcy.. 44

Practical Steps 44

Rule Four: **Learn To Avoid Borrowing** 47

Loan Is Not A Gift.. 47

Credit Card... 49

Pay Later Bait.. 50

"Ajo System" an Alternative 52

Wait! 53

Rule Five : **Learn To Be Content**................................ 58

Need Or Want?.. 59

Self-Control... 62

How To Practice Contentment 65

Rule Five: **Learn To Be A Good Steward** 68

Avoid Waste.. 68

Good Work Ethic.. 74

Rule Seven: **Learn To Give**.. 78

Two Copper Coins.. 80

Lunch Pack.. 80

Last Dinner.. 81

Chocolate Box.. 82

Appendix 85

Dedication

I give thanks to my Lord Jesus Christ for giving me the knowledge and resources to make the publication of this book a reality.

I am grateful to David Gloin who assisted in proofreading the manuscript and agreed to endorse it with a foreword.

I would like thank Roland Haigh, the Chief Executive Officer of Citizens Advice Bexley for his encouragement and support in the writing of this book.

My thanks also go David Akinwusi the managing director of Davo Graph for his valuable contributions and the design of the inner and the cover pages of the book.

I express my profound gratitude to my former colleague Ray Wells who took time out of his retirement to proof read and offer invaluable professional advice.

I would like to thank my children: Oluwatosin and Ayomide for their support and suggestions.

Finally, to my soul mate, Adebisi who is always there for me day and night offering her suggestions, support and encouragement. Thank you!

Foreword

"Money makes the world go round" sings Sally Bowles and EMCEE in Cabaret. Well it does; much more flexible than bartering; but it can bring everything to a grinding halt if not managed well. We have recent memory of the mess governments, central and commercial banks made by lending and encouraging lending to those who could not afford to pay (and of the bailout paid for by those who had suffered most through taxes and cutbacks).

From his considerable experience as a money adviser and his deep Christian faith Femi Adedayo in his second book is able to share great wisdom based on real experience in the management of money distilled into his Seven Cardinal Rules of Debt Avoidance.

Whether you are an individual, a couple or a family you need to manage your money - what you receive and what you pay out - to ensure you have the essentials of shelter, warmth, clothes and food and avoid your life (and those of your dependents) being derailed by debt collectors, bailiffs, evictions. If you are not "the breadwinner" you need to take responsibility for your spending and make whatever contribution (financial or otherwise) you are able.

For Femi, and for me, the Christian approach is essential. It is a fallacy that Christianity is just about what you do with your Sundays or tick boxing some aspects of your life. "Religion is a practical discipline [...requiring...] a dedicated lifestyle", it has to be lived to be valid. Lived out in every part of your life, including money, and every day – "seven whole days not one in seven" as the hymn writer puts it. So the faith infuses this approach to money and its management.

Christianity and this book is not about you not doing things, not enjoying life, not being happy, but about taking control in a way which enhances your life, allowing contentment and happiness to break in, providing purpose and hope for the future. Having explained the importance of Christianity to the author, this book is for everyone, those of other faiths and of none, because the issues, the principles Femi introduces and the benefits are universal.

So we are privileged that Femi has shared with us all that he has learned from his real life experience of helping people in financial distress and I commend this book to you, read it, ponder it but most importantly make it and its Seven Cardinal Rules part of your daily routine.

"My other piece of advice, Copperfield," said Mr. Micawber, "you know. Annual income twenty pounds, annual expenditure nineteen nineteen six, result happiness. Annual income twenty pounds, annual expenditure twenty pounds ought and six, result misery."

David B. Gloin
Preacher, Orpington & Chislehurst Circuit of the British Methodist Church UK
Christmas 2015

Preface

One thing you must realise and that is certain is that, whatever financial decision you make will have a significant impact on the remainder of your life from the point you make such decision.

Sometimes it may be easier to make money than to manage it. The National Endowment for Financial Education in America points to research that estimates of 70 per cent of people who unexpectedly come into large sums of money will lose it within seven years. This means that winning a lottery jackpot for example does not guarantee long-term financial security if not well managed.

This small book is the result of my own experiences over nine years in money advice. These self-acclaimed rules are tried and tested techniques and my intention is to make Money handling process simple by showing how these 'rules' can be applied practically to a real life situations. The aim of writing this book is to show you how to avoid pitfalls that may arise in money handling.

I have briefly discussed seven cardinal rules which in my opinion are a 'sine qua non' for anyone who wants to enjoy a financial freedom within their available resources. I believe if these rules are applied proactively to your day to day use and management of your money it will be of great assistance in the future.

Whatever effort you put in place in organising your finances to yield good result now and in the future.

I discovered that it might be difficult to totally separate the management of our money from Godly counsel, which are inherent in God's Word. Making a financial choice alone independent of God may be a disaster, hence the need to apply some godly counsel from the Scripture in support of some of the rules as discussed in this book. The Scripture says "…You may say in your heart, 'My power and the strength of my hand made me this wealth. But you shall remember the LORD your God, for it is He who is giving you power to make wealth that He may confirm His covenant which He swore to your fathers, as it is this day" (Deuteronomy 8:17-18). This is to confirm that there is no way we can separate the use and management of our money from the need of God's wisdom.

Rule One

Learn To

BUDGET

"A prudent man sees evil and hides himself, the naive proceed and pay the penalty" - Proverbs 27:12

"Planning is bringing the future into the present so you can do something about it now" - Alan Lakein

Rule One: Learn To Budget

Is there anyone here who, planning to build a new house, doesn't first sit down and figure the cost so you'll know if you can complete it? If you only get the foundation laid and then run out of money, you're going to look pretty foolish. Everyone passing by will poke fun at you: 'He started something he couldn't finish it'' – Luke 14:28

One day in the ant colony, the Queen said, "we shall be having a meeting tomorrow". She therefore instructed one of the Soldier Ants who works as the town crier to inform others about the meeting. The town crier took the gong and went to the street to make the public announcement about the meeting.

"What is the agenda of the meeting?" asked, the town crier. The Queen replied; we need to build a befitting palace that will be an envy of the community and the surrounding villages. Why do we need to have a meeting because we want to build a palace? Why can't we start building right away? said the Soldier Ant.

We need everybody's contributions and to also determine what it willcost to have a palace of our dream, replied the Queen. The Queen further said that, the Soldier Ant's idea to start building without costing is an idea but not a good one. She reminded the

. . . It will be a splendid decision if you can learn on how to plan your finances ahead as the ants did

Soldier Ant about their neighbouring village where Grasshopper lives and they are yet to complete their own palace because they had no adequate preparation and costing and they ran out of funds that led to the project has being abandoned.

The Soldier Ant agreed with the Queen and the meeting was held. At the meeting, costing was done, plans were made, and each Ant was given assignment to perform according to each Ant's ability. At the end a befitting palace of their dream was built within a record time.

It will be a splendid decision if you can learn on how to plan your finances ahead as the ants did.

Likewise, every driver knows the importance of having a roadmap or satellite navigator when taking a journey to a place where he has never been before.

"A sensible man watches for problem ahead and prepares to meet them. The simpleton never looks and suffers the consequences." - Proverbs 27:12 NTL

If he does not know where he is going, he may end up somewhere he does not want to be. Our financial future can be likened to a destination where we have not been and a direction is needed to get there. Budgeting to personal financial management is what sat nav or roadmap is to a driver who is taking a journey to an unchartered territory.

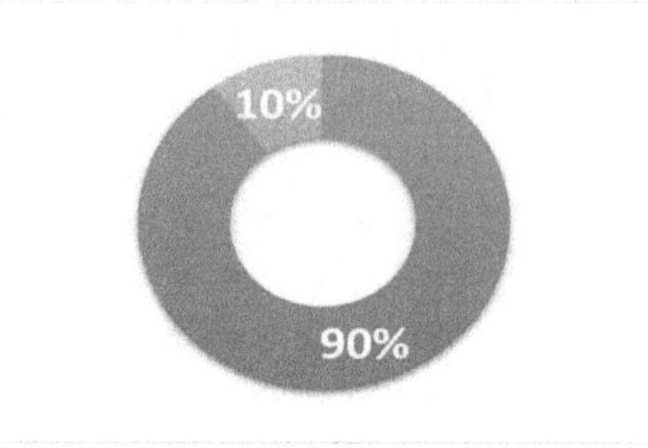

This rule states that 10% of time spent on planning and organising your work before you begin will save 90% of time in getting the job done once you get started. I can say that this rule is applicable to how your finances should be managed. Take some time to plan your finances by drawing up a personal budget before you begin to spend, preferably before you receive your income. Any quality time spent on planning is a valuable time that will be appreciated at the end.

We have a lot to learn from the life of the ants as it teaches us the importance of planning for the future needs and there is no better way to start than having a budget plan for management of our finances.

Though budgeting may not seem to be the most exciting thing to do, it is vital in keeping your financial house in order. Budgeting is not and should not be seen as an emotional decision on paper, but a financial plan based on reality. If you are to keep track of your finances, the best way to start is through budgeting. The Word of God admonished us that: "A sensible man watches for problem ahead and prepares to meet them. The simpleton never looks and suffers the consequences." – Proverbs 27:12. When you budget based on your actual income it will help you to live a lifestyle of reality. By this, you will avoid living in bondage of credit.

In the ancient Egypt during the reign of King Pharaoh Joseph, the prime minister, put a plan in place whereby a portion, one fifth (20%), of the abundance of grain harvested during the good years were stored up so that when the famine came, there was a plentiful supply to provide for all the food needs of the people of Egypt, and

In order to have an accurate budgeting, you must know or have an idea of how much money you spend weekly or monthly. You might find it useful to keep a note of all that you spend over a few weeks to get an estimate of your cash flow.

even for the many desperate people who came from other countries to purchase grain.

Having a budget will afford you a plan for the immediate and the future needs and spending. You will be able to compare your income with how much you are spending and adjust accordingly to meet your financial obligations.

Appropriate budgeting requires you to examine your needs against your wants – expenses that you can't avoid, spending that is optional.

In the story above, the Grasshoppers failed to complete their own palace because they did not have a plan to know how much it will cost them before embarking on the project. Hence, halfway when they ran out of funds; they did not have a 'plan B' on the way forward.

The first rule of budgeting is to spend less than you earn. If your total monthly income is £1500, then you should plan to spend less than £1500 in order to maintain a positive budget and to provide for the unexpected.

When you budget, it will help you to save money by planning ahead. To illustrate this with the story of Mr. Fish who buys a daily cup of coffee on the way to work for £2.50 at Coffee shop. "Mr. Fish, good morning", the shop attendant greeted. "Morning, Janet how are you today?" Mr. Fish enquired. "Fine, thank you. What are you having this morning?" Janet asked. "As usual, but with no sugar today because I am trying to cut down on my sugar intake as advised by the doctor", Mr. Fish said. Janet said, "Okay, no problem give me a minute".

One day Mr. Fish attended a half-day free seminar organised by his church where a money adviser was invited to talk about the importance of budgeting and savings. Having being touched by the outcome of the seminar, Mr. Fish took pen and paper and analysed one area of his spending, which is his daily intake of coffee on his way to work. Below is the outcome of his comparison if he were to be making the coffee himself rather than buying at coffee shop every morning.

	Daily	Weekly	Monthly	Yearly (48 Weeks)
Coffee Shop	£2.50	£12.50	£55.00	£600
Home Made	22p	£1.05	£4.67	£50.40
Savings	£2.28	£11.45	£50.33	£549.60

Mr. Fish was alarmed as he can see that a whopping sum of £549.60 would be saved annually if he prepares his own coffee. If you don't budget you may have no idea how much you are spending and how those little expenses affect your overall yearly expenditure. Budgeting can help you find and eliminate excessive or unnecessary spending.

you are spending and how those little expenses affect your overall yearly expenditure. Budgeting can help you find and eliminate excessive or unnecessary spending.

In budgeting, you should not forget to incorporate the following into your plans:

*Yearly Budget: You should make a plan for everything to be spent during the year based on the income for the year.

*Windfall Plan: You must propose beforehand what additional income will be spent on e.g. Annual Tax Refund. At the beginning of the year I always include my may be tax return in my budget as income, which is to be used as my holiday expenses for the year.

*Long Range Plan: Long range financial plan includes; wedding plan, saving for deposit for a new car, house, the arrival of a child either by birth or adoption.

You may get some money every week, fortnightly, four weekly and some monthly. When working out your budget decide whether you are working out your budget monthly or weekly. With the advent of various handheld mobile devices, it is very easy and convenient to draw up your budget. There are several applications (apps) on OS, Android, Windows platforms, which are available for free downloads on your phones and tablets. Make use of this and I believe that you will not regret doing so.

In the course of my job when I am assisting clients to draw up their financial statement (budgeting), there is always one common statement from some of them when extracting information about their expenses.

The statement is usually 'I have not thought of that, is that

---

"If you fail to plan, you are planning to fail"
— Benjamin Franklin

---

necessary?' This is when asked if they buy newspaper; subscribed to online newspaper, pay for parking, sometimes the cost of hairdo. Some of these spending and subscriptions may be as little as 99p or less but they still count towards your monthly expenditures.

How To Budget

1. Set a goal for what you want to achieve. This goal may range from saving for retirement, capital project, paying off debts etc.

2. Make sure your expectation is realistic. Don't budget on assumptions. I am very much aware that it may be difficult budgeting on a variable income. If you are self-employed, on a zero-hour contract, or you work on commission only. This is where you cannot predict how much money you will have coming each month. In this case, I will suggest that you always make extra provisions in your budget for savings in the months of surplus income knowing full well that some of your expenses are constant in each month.

3. List and calculate your income. This must include all sources – salary, welfare benefit, contributions from other family members and returns from investment such as interest from your savings account.

4. List and calculate your expenses. This must include rent, mortgage payment, council tax, utilities, car park charges, car insurance, bank charges etc.

5. Prioritise your expenses. From the list of your expenses you need to categorise them into priority and non-priority. Your priority expenses are those expenses that will provide you with basic necessities such as food, shelter, electricity, gas, child maintenance, sometimes payment to other family members you live with or are dependent upon you etc. While your non-priority expenses are the cost of eating out, socialising, pay tv, broadband smartphone and the cost, buying of newspapers and magazines etc.

6. Compute by subtracting your expenses total from the income total. The expectation is at least to have income equals expenses. However, the ultimate aim is to have a surplus income no matter how little. If this is not the case you may need to check your expenses to see if there are things to cut down. Also check your income list and be sure that nothing is left out.

You do not need to be a mathematician to do this, as there are free apps from your phone, tablet or computer. What you will only need to do is to enter these figures on your lists (income and expenses) to the appropriate columns it will work out the result for you. (see appendix for a pen and paper system).

7. Review your budget. It is very important that you sit down at a fixed time each week or month to review your budget on regular basis to be sure you are on track to achieving your budgeting goal. Likewise, on the same day each year review your budget

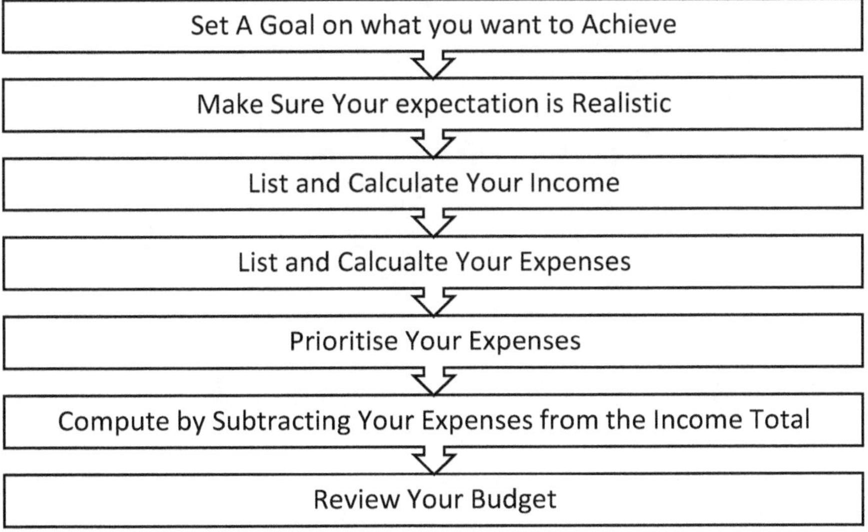

and change it to reflect changes in your income and your spending. Budget plan should not be static but dynamic.

Rule Two

Learn To

Save

"A wise man saves for the future, but the foolish man spends whatever he gets" - Proverbs 21:20 TLB

"Little drops of water, little gains of sand, make the pleasant land" – Julia Carney 1845

If Ant, You Can

One sunny afternoon in the summer, a Grasshopper, hopping about, saw Ant in the scorching sun working himself out toiling and gathering grains into the barn. The Grasshopper took time to stop and said to the Ant, "what is that you are doing? Why don't you join me and have a good time instead of toiling in this sun?"

"Thanks for the offer, "said the Ant. "As you can see I am helping to lay up food for the winter and it will be wonderful if you too can do the same". "Me?" the Grasshopper laughed in a scorning way, Why will I do that? When there are plenty of grains to eat now there is no need to store up for the winter, winter will take care of itself when it is time".
Ant continued with his toiling, gathering and storing grains into the store while the Grasshopper also went on his way.

When the winter came, and the cold was unbearable and no one could go out to work Ant never lack anything because of the savings he already had. Ant and the members of his household had plenty to eat from the grains stored during summer and were able to give to their neighbours. While the Grasshopper on the other hand, had no food to eat and he and his household were dying of hunger. He remembered his folly and that he has been a twit for not taking to the Ant's counsel and saved up food during summer.

"You can make a choice right away, from either learning from the Ant or follow the part of the Grasshopper."

Joseph's Savings Strategy

In the ancient Egypt, there was a time of severe famine, which lasted for seven years; the one-fifth of the savings was enough to sustain Egypt and other nations.

Pharaoh had a foreknowledge of what is going to happen in the first seven years of plenty and the subsequent seven years of famine through the interpretation of his dream, which was given to him by God through Joseph. However, he does not know what to do.

"Joseph, now that we know what is going to happen in the next fourteen years what shall we do? " Pharaoh enquired.

Joseph said, "Oh King, appoint officers over the land, to collect one-fifth of the produce of the land of Egypt in the seven plentiful years. And let them gather all the food of those good years that are coming, and store up grain under your authority and let them keep food in the cities".

"Also", Joseph continued; "then that food shall be as a reserve for the land for the seven years of famine, which shall be in the land of Egypt that the land may not perish during the famine".

Just as Joseph said, Egypt experienced seven years of plenty and when these were ended the seven years of famine began. However, despite the fact that the famine was in all lands; there was bread in Egypt because of the savings that were made during the period of plenty.

You may have to learn from the Ants by simply setting aside a portion of your current income for future use. That is, a portion of your disposable income not spent on consumption of consumer goods is put aside for the 'winter' season. Developing a rich and rewarding saving culture isn't something you accomplish overnight; you have to work at it with absolute determination. But, I can assure that, the rewards are more than worth the effort.

If you are finding it difficult to save, you're not alone; everybody struggles in this. However, those who succeed are those who learn to put concerted effort in self-discipline and determination to do it no matter what it cost which includes self-denial.

Funds kept aside, will help you to be financially secure in case of unexpected change in your circumstances such as loss of job or business, ill health, national or global economic meltdown or recession. It has been said that to be financially secure during the time of financial difficulty, an individual or household should save at least six months' worth of expenses. For example, if you spend

£1,000 monthly on expenses, you should therefore have at least £6,000 in savings. Therefore, work towards having at least these savings at the end of your monthly cost.

Pay yourself first has been a popular and very effective saving strategy that has been helping individual's saving habit over spending. This strategy means that you set aside a portion of your income before you start to spend the rest. However, for Christian believers, I would say that you pay yourself second. The first payment should always go to God the owner of the resources by paying your tithe, which should at least be 10%. God is the major shareholder of the investment and He must be paid first. Therefore, I recommend that your tithe should be incorporated in your budget.

I understand that your income may be low but it is possible to save at least 20 pence if only you can sacrifice on non-essential expenditures such as a daily newspaper and keep the cost as your savings. With 20 pence a day savings at the end of the year you would have saved £73. For those that their income is from social welfare benefit and most of the time there's usually nothing left, it doesn't mean you can't save. You may not be able to control how much you receive on weekly, bi- weekly or monthly basis but you have and can control what goes out of your account. That is, you can change how much you spend on non-essentials to give you room for little savings. You will never know how this will work until you start.

When I was growing up in my town in Nigeria, I used to watch how the street market adjacent to our house which always start with one seller setting stall, then become full with both sellers and buyers within a space of half an hour.

One after the other; the market becomes full not as an influx but with incoming of one or two persons after the other. Nobody waits until the market is full before coming to buy or sell.

You don't have to have a big income before you can cultivate the habit of saving, start from one penny if that is what you could afford to save and add another penny later, it will surprise you that within a space of time you will have a pound in your savings. Remember the more your income the more your expenses and wants will be.

In order to save you must first make it a habit. By the time you start it and do it regularly, you'll quickly find that your little pounds each week or months add up and keep growing. By inculcating the saving habit into your lifestyle, you will be earning interest rather than paying interest if you were to be borrowing.

There was a time that I realised that most of the TV channels we view on our cable TV (Sky Subscription) are available on Freeview channels. As these available channels are more than enough to view I decided to cancel my monthly TV subscription of £21. We did not have subscription for 3 years and we never regretted it instead we have £756 as savings. This saving did not come as a result of windfall or increase in income but out of the income we already had. It came from reprioritising our needs by cutting our non-essential expenses. This is why I believe that anyone can save if one's mind is set at it.

Some of my clients are usually surprised when a token offer of £1 a month is proposed and accepted by their creditors. I usually explain to them that their creditors are wise to accept the £1 a month offer.

If they have 10,000 customers who are repaying 'bad debts' at the rate of £1 a month, they are not receiving £1 but £10,000 monthly which is far better than nothing. They understood the statement "Little drops of water, little grains of sand, make the mighty ocean and the pleasant land". - Julia Carney 1845. If this is applied to how you save you will be surprised how quickly a few pounds each month builds up!

The importance of savings cannot be overemphasised. Your savings will be very handy in case of emergency (rainy-day) when you need to replace a broken appliance such as the washing machine or the gearbox of the car. Savings will help in the event of losing your job or being off work sick without pay.

In the story of the Ant and Grasshopper I shared previously, we can see that both the Ant and Grasshopper experienced a very harsh winter, but Ant did not suffer because of the stock he has put in store during summer.

The first few months of buying our home on mortgage were very difficult for us to save as we used to; simply because our mortgage monthly repayment is times two of our previous rent cost. Also, we needed to buy some household utensils, sofas and bedding.

However, I realised that if our salaries were to be delayed by a day we will be in default of our mortgage repayment because we do not have savings that are accessible to pay for a month.

Though we make monthly savings to what we call 'Retirement Pot' that is not for emergency and not cashable as it is for retirement purposes. Therefore, we have to quickly adjust our budget and make some cut downs in order to start to save again. I remember what the Bible says in Proverbs 6:6-8 "Take a lesson from the ants, you lazy fellow. Learn from their ways and be wise! For though they have no king to make them work, yet they labour hard all summer, gathering food for the winter."

If you think that you don't have enough to start with a standing order or direct credit from your current account to savings account.

Coin Jar

You can start at your 'Home Bank' with the traditional piggy bank. I remember some years ago, we had this plastic coin jar at home where we drop the brown coins (1p & 2p). Towards the end of the year we took the coin jar to a local supermarket coins machine where the total coins amounted to about £40, which was more than enough for Christmas turkey.

Saving at home may be a starting point. The aim is to be able to take it further to benefit from saving interest that is available in Credit Union, Banks and Building society and savings accounts.

Clearance Sales

One of the ways we have managed to reduce our household spending is to take advantage of genuine sales wherever possible. We usually buy our Christmas gifts a year ahead during sales. We buy Christmas wrappers and crackers in January to be used the next Christmas.

In buying clothes for the family, it is advisable to plan your spending in advance and do not over purchase. Where possible, buy winter clothes in summer and summer clothes in the winter in this way you will make some savings. Try and avoid current season clothes' lines in stores. There is nothing current about them in the next few weeks; they will become past season lines when their price tag would have changed and reduced while their quality remain the same.

Do It Yourself

When we discovered that we practically have nothing left to save at the end of the month after meeting all our financial commitments. We began to check our spending and we realised that we could save money by washing our car by ourselves at home. We usually spend

£12 per wash at the car wash and washing the car twice in a month means that we spend £24 monthly. Assuming that the water and soap we now use cost £8 that means that we will be saving £16 a month and £192 a year.

The way to start saving is very simple and not burdensome at all. If you have some cash available called "disposable income" at the end of the month after all your essentials have been taken care of, then try to save it. Make a decision at onset to save at least 5% of your income and the more you are able to save, the better.

Let us take for example: Toto, who works with a publicity firm, earns £1,200 a month. After paying for all her essentials she has cash available of £180. Toto, who has decided at the beginning that she will save 5% of her income, works out that 5% which is £60, and puts this into a savings account every month. This means she will then have £120 (£180 minus £60) to spend on non-essentials, like going out. Over a year, Toto would have put £720 into her savings.

Shop Around

Another way to save is to shop around. To shop around simply means to go from one store to another store in search of merchandise or bargains. This is a process, which may require a little pain, which may eventually bring you gains.

It is a simple process of comparing goods and prices and considers various possibilities before making a choice. It does not matter what your purchasing power may be or how little or big the commodity you want to purchase.

Shopping for a financial product, be it a mortgage, services such as banking or a builder is no different to buying a TV, holiday, bread, milk and a can of coke. To get the best deal, you need to compare what's on offer from different companies. The word of God describes a prudent woman that; You never know how much you can be saving with buying a product that is 10p cheaper until you buy ten of such product weekly over a period of one year. Take your note pad and pen and let us do the calculation [(10p X 10) x 52 weeks = £52]. This means that you are £52 richer in a year which can be added to your savings for the year.

I went to a store to buy body cream and on getting there the retail price for one was £5. As usual, I checked other stores before making my final decision to buy. I entered the next store, which happened to be the high-end store. The same product with the same contents and weights is being sold for £3 each. I therefore bought four for £12 rather than buying only two for £10 at the previous store.

The journey to the store took me less than a minute walk. This means that by taking the pain to walk few steps to other store I have saved £2 on each bottle. Two pounds may not be much but if I have to save this each month at the end of the year I would have saved £24.

Christmas Club

There is no gain-saying that Christmas period is one of those periods when expenses shoot-up as a result of buying gifts, food and drinks either for friends and family or colleagues. It is a good idea if you can find a Christmas Savings Club agency in your area where you can save in advance for Christmas spending.

Christmas club is one of the ways to save for Christmas expenses. This is a type of scheme where a certain amount is put aside regularly each month at the beginning of the year. In most cases you may not have access to the savings until a few weeks before Christmas. Also, depending on the type of the scheme you sign to, you may not receive physical cash to spend but gift vouchers or gift cards which are acceptable at major retailers. In another, you may have to buy goods and services directly from the club. It is a good idea to check before you join.

All in all, you still have the advantage of having money to spend during the festive period without necessarily have to borrow or dip into other savings. However, you have to be careful because of the risk involve where a Christmas savings club goes bust as you may lose your savings.

Tips on how to save

- Set a goal and on how much of your income you want to save.
- Set up a direct credit to your savings account if you have one.
- Remove luxuries from your list of expenditures such as optional television channels subscriptions
- Start savings at the minimum of 10% of your income and have a plan to increase the percentage going forward.
- Save for future needs than to rely on credit.
- Cut down on non-essential expenses
- Food - "Don't shop when you are hungry"
- Shopping around - You do not have to be a loyal customer at your own detriment.
- You may wish to consider utility savings stamps
- Voluntary Christmas Club

Rule Three

Learn To

Pay Your Debt

"Pay to all what is owed to them: taxes to whom taxes are owed, revenue to whom revenue is owed, respect to whom respect is owed, honour to whom honour is owed" – Romans 3:7

"Some debts are fun when you are acquiring them, but none are fun when you set about to retiring them" – Ogden Nash

The story of a widow was told in the Bible whose husband was owed money to a creditor before he died. The creditor came threatening to take the widow's two sons as slaves if her husband's debt is not paid. The encountered of this woman with Elisha, the prophet of God produced a very remarkable miracle of abundance. The little jar of oil the woman had became many pots and pans of oil which she was instructed to sell and pay her debts first, and she and her two sons live on the rest.

This widow was advised to pay her debts first because if the debts were still outstanding, she and her sons will still be susceptible to creditor's harassment. Not until the debts were paid, she would not know her real financial worth.

I will like to make the following suggestions, which I believe will be helpful when dealing with your debts. These are suggestions and by all means you may not have to take them, as these are not exhaustive some may not be applicable to your own situation.

I have discovered that borrowing more money to pay debts is not always a good idea in dealing with debts, as this most of the time will plunge you into more debts. Sometimes your bank may suggest to you to consolidate your debts. This may seem to be an attractive way of dealing with your debts by arranging another loan for you but you may end up in a worse position. The loan your bank is offering you is just a way of transferring your debts and it is neither paying off the debts nor reducing it.

In order to avoid 'financial punishment' from your creditors, it is advisable to contact your lenders or creditors immediately you foresee that payment will be missed. This is very important that you contact your creditors and inform them about your inability to meet your credit commitment. There may be ways by which you can be helped by your lenders or creditors without being penalized for late or missed payments. For example, you may be offered a holiday period on your mortgage payment or personal loan, which means that recovery procedure, may be suspended for a period of time to give you a breathing space to organize your finances.

It is difficult to overstate the spectacular benefits of having savings. However, it will be a very foolish scale of value or priority to have savings when you have debts outstanding unless the savings goal is to pay off the debts owed.

If you have overdraft, loan or credit card at the same time you have savings in your account. It is better to pay off your debts than keeping the money in your savings account. This is because the amounts you earn or receive on your savings are always far less than the amount you pay in interest on your borrowings. But keep saving what you can. Using your savings to pay off your borrowing could save you hundreds of pounds a year in interest charges.

Let us illustrate it this way: If Mr. Jones had £1,000 debts on his credit card at 18%, the interest cost will be £180 per annum. At the same time if he had £1,000 in his savings at 2%, the interest that earned after tax will be £20. If his debt is paid off with his savings, he will be £160 a year better off.

Therefore, overall, it'll always cost more to borrow in whatever disguise than you can earn by saving. However, the only reason why you may want to save than to pay your debt may arise if paying off the debts incurs penalty e.g. paying off mortgages. In this case, you may leave the cash sitting in a savings account until the penalty is small enough that it doesn't matter and would not cost you more.

We have discussed this at the beginning of this book. See how much of your available cash can be offered to your creditors to pay off your debts. Work out how much you can afford to pay. There are several budget tools available as discussed in the first chapter that can help work out how much money you have to pay towards your debts.

Prioritize your debts.

Give priority to those debts, which have grave consequences for not paying them. Priority debts are the outstanding that should be paid first. These aren't necessarily the largest debts or the debts with the highest interest rate, but they are priority because of the severe consequences of not paying them.

Example of priority debts and their severe consequences for non-payment:

Type of debt	Consequences of non-payment
Mortgage or secured loan	Repossession
Rent	Eviction
Council Tax	A visit from bailiffs, money taken from wage, money taken from benefits, debt secured against home, bankruptcy, imprisonment
Child Maintenance	Money taken from wage, money taken from benefits, visit from bailiffs, imprisonment
Magistrates Court Fines	A visit from bailiffs, money taken from wage, money taken from benefits, imprisonment
Tax, VAT or National Insurance	A visit from bailiffs, money taken from wage, bankruptcy, County Court judgment (CCJ)
County Court judgment	A visit from bailiffs, a charging order, money taken from wage
TV licence	A fine
Gas or electricity	Disconnection, money taken from benefits
Hire purchase or logbook loan	Repossession, County Court judgment (CCJ)
Telephone	Disconnection, County Court judgment (CCJ)

While 'Non-Priority' debts include:

- Personal loans
- Credit cards
- Overdrafts
- Store cards
- Catalogue debts
- Payday loans

- Cancelled contracts e.g. old mobile phone debts

'Square peg Debts'

There are some debts that can be said to be 'Square peg Debts'. They are called 'square peg' debts because they do not fit neatly into the priority or non-priority debt categories. For example, a hire purchase may be a non-priority in many cases but, non-payment of hire purchase payments may lead to the repossession of the goods to which they relate. If, for example, this was a car that is essential to get to work, then losing it may have serious consequences. Therefore, hire purchase can be either priority or non-priority depending on individual circumstances.

When in financial difficulty, it is wise to seek help from organizations you don't have to pay to deal with your debts for you. Some of these organizations are run by charities that are willing to advise you and negotiate with your creditors on your behalf and make repayment arrangement for you. Some of these organizations can provide this service free of charge and others may charge setup fees as well as ongoing monthly charges.

There are options available to you in dealing with your debts especially if you have money left to offer your creditors. *(These options are applicable to England and Wales in the United Kingdom)* **Some of these options are as follows:**

Negotiation

This is an option where you work out your offers of payment based on a pro-rata equitable distribution of your disposable income. Disposable income is the amount you have available after you have taken away your essential expenses from your income. Also, you have worked out what you have to pay any priority debts. In this case, you have to make arrangement on how to pay your creditors individually.

Full and Final Payment

Full and Final Settlement: This means that you ask your creditors to let you pay a lump sum instead of the full balance you owe on the debt. In return for having a lump-sum payment, the creditor agrees to write off the rest of the debt. Example: Jane owes a total debt of £7,000 and offers a lump sum of £4,500 as full and final settlement. If her creditor agreed; the balance of £2,500 will be written off, which means she does not have to pay the balance again.

Debt Management Plan

This is an agreement between you and your creditors to pay all of your debts. You make regular payments to a licensed debt management company. The company shares this money out between your creditors on pro-rata basis. You make one monthly repayment to Debt Management Company (DMC) instead of multiple payments to each creditor. Then the DMC makes payments to your creditors on your behalf on pro-rata basis. This is not a legally binding arrangement as creditors can continue with their recovery procedures.

Administration Order

An administration order is a way to deal with debt if you have a county court or High court judgement against you and you can't pay in full. The debt must be less than £5,000. You make one payment a month to your local court. The court will divide this money between your creditors

Individual Voluntary Arrangement

This is a legally binding agreement with your creditors to pay all or part of your debts. The IVA consumer protocol guidelines suggest a minimum of three or more lines of credit from two or more creditors. In IVA, you will agree to make regular payments to an insolvency practitioner, who will divide this money fairly between your creditors. This can also be a one-off payment known as a lump sum IVA. Where payments are made in affordable monthly, it is usually lasts five or six years after which any remaining debt is written off at the last payment. You may have to pay for charges for advice and cost for running the IVA.

Debt Relief Order

Where you do not have money left and you don't think your financial situation will improve in the shortest possible time, you may wish to consider Debt Relief Order (applicable in England) or Bankruptcy.

Debt relief order or Bankruptcy is not a step to be taken lightly as the consequences are serious. You may lose assets and your ability to get credit in the future will be affected for several years.

Bankruptcy

Bankruptcy is a legal process which happens when a person or an organisation does not have enough money to pay all its debts. The process may be different from one country to another. At the end the person is free from the debt, but he may find it difficult to borrow money in the nearest future.

Practical Steps

- Sort out how much money you owe.

- Work out which are the most urgent debts for you to pay off.

- Work out if you've got any money after cutting non-essential expenses to pay your debts off and, if so, how much.

- Deal with the most urgent debts as a matter of priority.

- Look at your options for dealing with the less urgent debts and work out how to pay them off.

- Contact your creditors and make arrangements to pay back what you owe.

- Work out your options if you don't have enough money to pay off all your debts.

- Check your bills and statements especially bank credit / debit card statements as they come and challenge items which do not look correct.

- Some of these options will involve you paying charges and fees reducing the amount you have available to reduce your debts; so check before you decide which option to take.

Rule Four

Learn To

Avoid

Borrowing

"Dry crumbs in peace are better than a full meal with strife."
- Proverbs 17:1.

"A creditor is worse than a slave-owner; for the master owns only your person, but a creditor owns your dignity, and can command it." - Victor Hugo

Loan Is Not A Gift

"Good day Tom, guess what happened today", Kevin said enthusiastically. "No, give me the gist", Tom said. "I am on top of the moon, as I speak to you now. I am just returning from my bank as a lucky man. The bank has granted my personal loan of £5,000 payable in 60 months instalments", Kevin explained beaming with smile. "Really? How I wish I were as lucky as you are", Tom lamented.

Just like Kevin, some people take pride in being able to obtain loan or credit card as if they are free. Loans, overdrafts and credit cards are obligations, which must be fulfilled at a price in the future. It is a very wrong mind-set and assumption to think that you are being lucky or enjoying favour when your loan or credit card application is being approved.

Don't get me wrong; there are things that you may need to get a loan for such as education and housing. To me, these two can be seen as investment and acquisition of asset as rather than liabilities as they may be able to pay for themselves in the future. My understanding is that Payday loan and credit card will neither buy you a house nor pay your university fees.

Learn not to borrow for any reason, if you can help it. It is commonly believed that it is good common sense to borrow and invest it either in the stock market or property market, but it is not always a good idea to borrow in order to speculate.

Nothing appreciates forever, not even houses. Houses appreciate artificially because of the availability of cheap credit. The 2008 recession experience was a proof that the highly prized investment can fail.

I understand that we may need assistance to undertake capital project such as buying a house, starting a business or sometimes buying a new car where it is absolutely necessary for our job, business or family use. In such cases there may not be too many options than to borrow. What I am saying is that, where borrowing is unavoidable, such as buying a house or a new car, try to make as big a down payment (deposit) as possible. The more of the cost of the purchase you can cover up front, the quicker you'll pay off your loan and the less you'll spend on interest. Put the payments in your budget plan as discussed in chapter one. Also, it is advisable to be sure that you have the means to keep the repayments otherwise you may end-up being in debt and may be losing your car or home.

My candid opinion is that we should learn not to borrow especially where it involves consumer goods such as clothing or household gadgets that are not necessary. For example, I have seen people taking credit to purchase new tablets while the old one they have is in perfect working condition and the reason for the new purchase was simply because it is a new edition or latest model. There was a newspaper report where half of adults admit being addicted to smartphone.

You must know that loan is a loan and not a gift and it must be paid back invariably with interest and sometimes plus charges. One of the mistakes that people who are already in debts make is that getting a loan will help them with their financial difficulties. Unfortunately, borrowing more money to pay off debt is like throwing fuel on a fire. Virtually all of the clients I have encountered who took loans or credit cards to pay off their existing debts regretted for doing so as this made their situation worse off.

If you are poor or your only source of income is from social welfare benefit and you are having financial difficulties, getting a payday loan, in pawnshop will not help you. Payday loan as an option in debt situation will plunge you into more debts. No matter how low you are financially, getting a payday loan or credit card will make it worse for you, as this will not help you at long run. Additionally, a loan sometimes may seem to be a buffer, which will not last long. It can also be like given someone a pain relief for an injury. If the root cause of the injury itself is not treated when the pain relief medicine will wear off and you will need another in 3 to 4 hours.

Credit Card

One of the most popular ways of borrowing is through credit card. With credit cards you can choose how much to spend out of your credit limit and how much to repay each month. You may win the argument why credit card is a good way of borrowing because of the benefit of the protection afforded by credit card users by United Kingdom legislation under section 75 of the Consumer Credit Act 1974. Under this Act, when you use your credit card to buy something more than £100 and up to £30,000, you get extra protection if something goes wrong with your purchase. This has been made popular and accepted way of shopping with the advent of E-commerce, which is the fastest growing retail, market in the world today. In recent years, online purchase account for about 19% of UK retail sales.

In as much as credit cards may offer you protection in some purchases, it is pertinent to note that it is still a form of borrowing (buy now and pay later), and the risk it brings with it cannot be ruled out. If you don't pay off your balance in full each month, or use a credit card to get cash ("free" hole in wall machine), you will start to accumulate interest at a relatively high rate. Therefore, if not curbed immediately, your debt can quickly get out of hand particularly if you pay off only the minimum monthly amount.

Let me illustrate it this way: John has a current outstanding balance of £1000 on his credit card at the rate of 30% APR, and the typical minimum repayment is 5%. It will take John eight years and two months to repay the balance in full in addition to the cost of repayment of £709.

If you are only taking the protection advantage that or convenience credit cards offer, you must be disciplined enough to control your spending habit as discussed under self-control. Pay the wholebill each month by the deadline. Many today are trapped in credit card debts under the pretext of protecting their purchases.

Pay Later Bait

Beware of "Nothing to pay until" or "No Interest" which may hide rolled up interest or payment protection insurance or higher interest rates.

According to Joyce Brothers: "Credit buying is much like being drunk. The buzz happens immediately, and it gives you a lift. The hangover comes the day after". Living on credit has been made so attractive and tempting that if you are not careful you will think that you are getting it for nothing. Beware of the trap of buy now and pay later plan that are being offered by stores. Ogden Nash says: "Some debts are fun when you are acquiring them, but none are fun when you set about to retiring them"

Louise decided to buy a new TV and walks in to a store on the high street. Louise does not have cash on her and does not have money in account either and wanted the TV. On the tag on the TV it says buy today and pay only £18.25 monthly.

Louise could not believe her eye and what she is reading, only £18.25 a month? "This is a bargain, I must go for it", she said quietly in her mind.

Louise approached the salesman at the store who explained to her how it works. The TV valued £450 at 29.9% APR (fixed) and make 36 months (3 years) payments of £18.25, and Louise will be making a total repayment of £656.91. Because of the excitement of having a new TV Louise did not check the terms and conditions of the credit and the penalties for default payments. Louise may not immediately realise that, the total repayment of £656, is about 50% more than the value of the TV. The attraction to Louise is the £18.25 a month and a brand new 50in TV when she has a 32in TV at home that is in good working condition.

Before you commit yourself to this type of purchase like Louise, you may wish to ask yourself do you really need 50in TV when you are not planning to turn your living room into a public cinema.

It does not matter the level of your borrowing. A borrower is servant to the lender. Those who live beyond their means by borrowing always end up being enslaved to their creditors.

"Ajo System" an Alternative

There are alternatives to borrowing if only we can be patient enough to look within. I remember when I was growing up in the part of the western of Nigeria region in the seventies through to eighties. There was no bank available and there were no cheap credit facilities available either. The only borrowing option available was through loan shark lenders. Does that mean that people were not involved in capital projects? Does that mean people were not involved in businesses that required large sums of money? If people were involved in capital projects and business how were they doing it without borrowing?

There was and there still are traditional ways by which money is raised for capital projects and big businesses. This is called 'AJO' in Yoruba society in Nigeria. AJO is a system by which people of like minds come together with one aim of raising money to assist one another. How does it work? I will give an example to illustrate how this system works. If five people agreed to contribute £1,000 a month let say from January that will create a pot of £5,000 a month. At the end of January one of the members called 'A' who is the first person on the list will be given the lump sum of £5,000. The list would have been created by cast a lot at the beginning. In February the next member on the list will be given

£5,000. This means that by the end of May every member in the group would have had a turn at the pot interest free. This system will not only help to make a compulsory savings, you will also have access to a lump sum of money at your disposal without any interest or charges. You can only imagine the phenomenal benefits of this if continued on a rollover basis in two years.

I can say categorically that I have been a beneficiary of this system in the past and I am still very favourably dispose to it even now. Some may want to argue that this is a primitive idea in this age and time. But I will say that you are totally wrong. It is the same system that banks are using the only difference is that they adapted it in order to make money out of it for themselves. Savings are collected from several customers and put in a pot and give the lump sum to corporations as loans for interest which is always higher than the marginal interest they pay depositors, that is if there is interest at all especially if the money is in current accounts.

Wait!

The world is in this trouble today because people don't want to wait. Most of debt problems are directly linked to the availability of credit.

When you wait for something you appreciate and value it more.

The Word of God says "Desire without knowledge is not good, and whoever makes haste with his feet misses his way" – Proverbs 19:2. Many times when we want something urgently, it could be a new sofa or a car, we don't bother to read the small print in the finance agreement before we sign the dotted lines and sometimes we find ourselves entering into an irrevocable agreement which later lands us into debt.

"No road is too long to the man who advances deliberately and without undue haste; and no honors are too distant for the man who prepares himself for them with patience."
- Jean de la Bruyere

I remember when we wanted a new car. My wife and I agreed to save for it rather than buying the car on finance. We saved for three years before we could buy a used car that was 3 year old. The good news is that we have no cause to have anxiety over missing monthly repayments to car finance company. Also, we are so favoured that the car has never given us any problem for the past 5 years we have been driving it. We had the option of not waiting for three years as we have good credit rating and we can walk into any garage and a finance car be arranged for us. But at what cost? When you do not want to wait and save up for what you want, and you borrow, it simply means you are bringing spending forward and you must realise that this will cost you.

I understand that there are situations that you may not be able to save up to buy certain things you need because it will take too long to do so. As I illustrated with my example of our saving for 3 years for a car, in your own case you may need the car now for work and may not be practicable to wait for that long. I know that cars do wear out, what I am saying is that if you need another car, it will be a good option to buy a good used car, preferably at a price that can be paid for without financing.

In all cases you may need to do the cost and benefit comparative analysis before settling for an option of what you want to do. One thing you must realise and that is certain is that, whatever financial decision you make will have a significant impact on the reminder of your life from the point of making such decision.

If you must extricate yourself from debt, the first principle is to learn not to have one and the way not to have one is by learning not to borrow.

Rule Five

Learn To be

Content

"Having food and raiment let us be therewith content" - - 1Timothy 6:8

"You say, 'If I had a little more, I should be very satisfied.' You make a mistake. If you are not content with what you have, you would not be satisfied if it were doubled."
- Charles H. Spurgeon

Rule Five : **Learn To Be Content**

Recently in UK, a 22-year-old man made a bankruptcy petition after spending over £100,000 on cosmetic surgery, designer outfits and jewellery. The cosmetic was not to correct any abnormality in him but for him to look like someone else. He spent thousands of pounds sterling trying to live the lifestyle of celebrities. This is what discontent lifestyle can lead to.

You must find contentment to some extent in the area of your looks if you must enjoy financial blaze. Many today are displeased with the way they look not because they have any physical deformity but because they want to look like someone else. Also some suffer from psychological disorder called body dysmorphic disorder, which means they see themselves or parts of their body as 'ugly' when they are actually quite normal or even look good.

It is now an open secret that borrowing money for cosmetic surgery is one of the biggest reasons for people getting into debt. 'Vanity medicine' procedures such as face lifts, breast augmentation, abdominoplasty (tummy tuck) and liposuction which are non-health related issues are daily being bought by those who are discontented with their looks and cost them lots of money. Unfortunately, these procedures are being financed through credit cards, bank loans, bank overdrafts and sometimes payday loans. Recently, a newspaper article suggested each of us spent over £90 on beauty products yearly.

Need Or Want?

You must be able to differentiate between needs and wants. You may not need the latest automobiles, electronic gadget and fashion. What you see and consider as latest today becomes out of fashion and obsolete tomorrow. You can never catch up with the fashion or science and technology worlds. To experience financial sovereignty and avoid debt, you must learn to be content with what you have.

It has been said that the average new car will have a residual value of around 40% of its new price after 3 years (assuming 10,000 miles per year) or, in other words, will have lost around 60% of its original value at average of 20% per year. This means that if you buy a new car for £10,000 and it might cost you £2,000 a year depreciation and be worth around £4,000 after 3 years. You will agree with me that within that space of 3 years the manufacturer would have brought out other latest models of the said make and brand. If your old car is in good working condition, why do you need the new model? Why not content with the one you have? However, if you're spending more to maintain your old car it will make economic sense to consider probably buying another car not necessarily the latest model.

However, if you must have a new car may be because of the type of job you do why you don't consider leasing rather than outright purchase. It may seem expensive but at long run it may work out cheaper for you.

In this case you pay a fixed monthly amount for the car, which generally includes servicing and repairs, but deals may vary so check the contract terms and conditions to make sure it suits you before you sign. This may work out to be the cheapest option, particularly if you cover a lot of miles.

A dictionary defines contentment as a disposition of mind in which our desires are confined to what we enjoy without murmuring at our lot, or wishing ardently for more. It is a state of mind in which you are satisfied with what you have.

Contentment does not mean you should not aspire to have better things than those you have now. It only implies that, your desires of wants be moderated that you do not indulge in acquisition of non-essentials through credit rather be content with what is affordable, reasonable and necessary. Many today are discontented, not because they are not doing well financially, but because they believe others are doing better than them.

Reading the Scriptures, a man called Apostle Paul knew the secret of contentment when he said: "I know what it is to be in need, and I know what it is to have plenty. I have learned the secret of being content in any and every situation, whether well fed or hungry, whether living in plenty or in want." - Philippians 4:12

According to the Bible, King Solomon in the ancient Israel, who can be considered as the wisest and richest man who ever lived, said something about man's insatiable desires.

This is applicable to the love of automobiles, fashion etc. You can never be satisfied in acquiring them if you are not content with the ones you have.

Dear friend, do you know that you don't have to do things or acquire goods in order to impress your neighbour, colleagues or your neighbour or your family members? The unfortunate part is that most of the time people you are trying to impress (which must have plunged you into debt) may not notice what you are using to impress them.

Dear friends, if you do don't have contentment; you may end up in servicing your appetite for the latest models with credit. While fashion houses are smiling to the bank with large profits, you may end up with the burden of debt.

In the Bible when God provided food for the children of Israel in the wilderness He instructed them to get manna according to their need and when they obeyed no one had lack and nothing was a waste.

However, some of the children of Israel did not heed Moses warning that they should not leave any of the manna till morning. Those who left part of it until morning discovered that it bred worms and stank. These people were afraid thinking that they may not have anything to eat the following day and were not content in what has been provided for them.

This does not negate the fact that we can make provision for the rainy day as I discussed in the previous chapter on learning to save. In the same chapter sixteen when they were commanded to take manna for the following day being a Sabbath, that manna did not stink and there were no worms in it.

We should be content with our daily bread and try to live on cash rather than on credit. The food supplied comes morning by morning in God's time in accordance to His plan.

Self-Control

You don't have to buy everything that you desire. When you walk into a shopping mall, there will be a lot of things that you fancy and are inviting. They are good, beautiful to behold, but may not be necessary and needful.

Having self-control in relation to the use of money will help to ensure that you are effectively managing your money in a way that will help in avoiding unnecessary and wasteful use of your hard-earned income. It will be one of the wisest decisions you would ever

"For the drunkard and the glutton shall come to poverty:
and drowsiness shall clothe a man with rags."
- Proverbs 23:20-21a

made if you could be more disciplined and focus on your priority needs rather than the 'nice to have' items.

The nature of man is to give in to the demand of his flesh. I mean a natural man obeys the dictates of his body; he gives to his body whatever the body wants sometimes at the expense of his health. One of the major causes of obesity today is indulgence in eating habits. We want to eat everything that we can lay our hands on.

We may also have bloated expenses if we do not control the way we satisfy our wants. We must be able to differentiate between wants and needs, between essential and desirable.

When we do, it will allow us to set our priority right. Even where things are needed and essential and the means are not available, ability to exercise self-control will go a long way not only in helping us to manage our resources, and it will prevent us from going into debt.

Where you do not have self-control you open the door to all kinds of temptation and become susceptible to falling into the schemes of the marketers who are ready to sell to you what you do not need. When you go to into the supermarket the first thing you see are the things that will attract your attention and sometimes not what will do you good. Also, as you are on your way to the till for payment you also have little things that you think that will not cost you much such as 60 pence candy or soft selling magazine. According to Benjamin Franklin "Beware of little expenses; a small leak will sink a great ship". You must make up your mind before going to the store what you intend to buy and where possible stick to it.

You may be able to avoid impulse buying if you do not go to stores or internet buying sites unless you really need to buy something you need. By doing this you will not put yourself in a situation where you might be tempted to spend money on non-essentials. I can say that I used to be guilty of this in the past when I go into store with the intention of 'window shopping' and end up coming out of the store with purchases, which ordinarily I shouldn't have bought.

The words of God says: "Then we will no longer be immature like children. We won't be tossed and blown about by every wind of new teaching. We will not be influenced when people try to trick us with lies so clever they sound like the truth." - Ephesians 4:14.

You should not allow stores to make you a chess pawn where you can be pushed around and tempted to buy things that are not needful.

When making a purchase decision you need to ask yourself some salient question such as is this item absolutely necessary? If not can I do without it? If not can I substantially reduce my spending?

According to Evening Standard newspaper dated the 26th of November 2015, half of Londoners who plan to hit the Black Friday sales admit they will buy items they don't need or want.

How To Practice Contentment

1. Develop a reasonable living style – even where you can afford things that are non-essentials it may not be necessary to buy them. You must have a disciplined attitude towards your wants.

2. Set firm priorities always – Don't allow things that are urgent take over things that are important. Sometimes things that are urgent may not be important.

3. Shopping List – Before you go for food or other shopping check your store cupboard and make a list of what you need. Then only buy those things.

4. Develop a thankful attitude – Give thanks for everything including your present financial position. In everything give thanks, for this is the will of God in Christ concerning you.

Rule Six

Learn To be A Good

Steward

"Now, a person who is put in charge as a manager must be faithful" –1Corinthians 4:2

"Abundance isn't God's provision for me to live in luxury. It's His provision for me to help others live. God entrusts me with His money not to build my kingdom on earth, but to build His kingdom in heaven"
– Randy Alcon

Avoid Waste

A visit to grocery stores a day preceding any bank holiday in the UK is usually unprecedentedly full with shoppers. Sometimes it seems as if there is going to be a war and every household should buy food that will last them till eternity. I visualise that supermarket trolley with a dozen liters of milk and a dozen large sliced loaves.

However, a day after the bank holidays, you will witness refuse bins on the street over filled with unwanted, spoiled and excess food that are being thrown away. I want to say that, every thrown away excess or unwanted food creates a hole in your finances.

In the Bible the miracle of the feeding of the five thousand by our Lord Jesus Christ was recorded. After everyone has eaten, filled and satisfied He instructed His disciples to pick the leftovers.

Though Jesus had power to provide any quantity of food, yet He has here taught us that the bounties of Providence are not to be squandered. In all things the Saviour set us an example of frugality, though He had an infinite supply at His disposal; He was Himself economical. He understands how to be a good steward of resources and set an example for you and I to follow.

According to Love food hate waste website almost 50% of the total amount of food thrown away in the UK comes from our homes. We throw away 7 million tonnes of food and drink from our homes every year in the UK, and more than half of this is food and drink we could have eaten. In translating this in monetary terms, wasting this food costs the average household £470 a year, rising to £700 for a family with children, the equivalent of around £60 a month.

A colleague of mine who went to superstore overheard a woman laden with clothes shopping say to her friend, "I won't wear most of this"!

Wastage may not be a deliberate attempt but you can make a deliberate decision to avoid it. You may start from avoiding water wastage by using a bucket to wash your car rather than using a hosepipe. Avoid energy wastage by switching off your electronic equipment from the main sockets when not in use. It is said that while electronic equipment are in standby mode they consume as much as 50% as they will ordinary consume while they are switch on.

Whenever wastage occurs from any aspect of life leads to waste of money and resources. When your electricity bills increase because of not switching off your appliances, this will result to increase in your monthly expenditure and decrease in your savings.

There is a popular story of a guy who is now famously known as the prodigal son in the Bible. I am very sure that was not the name his father would have given him at birth; because prodigal means wasteful.

In this story, this young man after he was given his inheritance gathered all and went to the city like our today's 'Las Vegas' and there he squandered all his wealth with loose living. This is the story in summary: "*...A man had two sons. The younger of them said to his father, 'Father, give me the share of the estate that falls to me.' So he divided his wealth between them, and not many days later, the younger son gathered everything together and went on a journey into a distant country, and there he squandered his estate with loose living. Now when he had spent everything, a severe famine occurred in that country and he began to be impoverished, so he went and hired himself out to one of the citizens of that country, and he sent him into his fields to feed swine. And he would have gladly filled his stomach with the pods that the swine were eating, and no one was giving anything to him.*" - Luke 15:11-16

That is what wastefulness could result in. That is the result of a bad steward of resources. This young man became bankrupt not because he does not have enough when he set out, but because he mismanaged his own inheritance.

If you are to stay out of debt, and enjoy financial freedom you must be a good steward of money. You must be prudent with the money at your disposal. Money must be spent sensibly. You must realise that you are the manager of your finances. Your faithfulness or unfaithfulness in the management of your finances will determine your prosperity or poverty. Where there is improper management of money, not only will you not have more, what you have will vanish.

This is another confirmation that money is from heaven and it returns to where it came from if not well managed.

A steward according to the dictionary is one who manages another's property, finances, or other affairs; one who administers anything as the agent of another or others. Stewardship in this context is not servanthood of money but a steward of God for the management of His resources which one of them happens to be the money at your disposal.

Let me quickly correct an impression before you get confused about why you are being regarded as a steward of your 'own money'. That is the point. What we tend to believe is that the money at our disposal is ours. "I work for my money and I can spend it the way I want and no question asked". That is where we are all wrong. Yes, it is true that you worked for the money, but remember that God makes it possible to be able to work. Many are fit, able and even more qualified than you but they wish they were able to work as you do. God plants the tree and causes it to produce fruits for you to pluck. The words of the Lord that says: "You might say in your heart, "The power and strength of my hands have made this wealth for me." *But remember that it is the LORD your God who gives you the power to gain wealth..."* - Deuteronomy 8:17-18a

God reminded Israel in the Bible that He owns everything. He says, "For all the animals of the forest are mine, and I own the cattle on a thousand hills. I know every bird on the mountains, and the world is mine and everything in it " - Psalm 50:10-11

God wants you to know that He owns everything including money you presume to have and the one you will yet have.

In order to experience financial freedom, you must handover the control of your money to God. When your money is under God's control, He will guide you in decision making on how to faithfully and judiciously utilise the resources.

We must see whatever resources we have as God's possession and we have been employed as managers who have been engaged to manage these resources to profit.

There three ways by which we can manage our finances, and each have different impact in our lives. Regardless of your income your spending lifestyle will usually fall in one of the categories below.

Spending Habit	What It Means	Impact	What to do
Above Your Means	<ul><li>Spending above your income and this means that you spending tomorrow's money today and tomorrow's money may not come.</li><li>Your income is less than your expenditures</li></ul>	<ul><li>Increase Debts</li><li>Family Tension</li><li>Harassed by debt collectors</li></ul>	<ul><li>Control your spending by budgeting and try to keep to it.</li><li>Where possible don't use credit cards.</li></ul>
Within Your Means	<ul><li>What you have is what you spend.</li><li>Your income equals your expenditures</li></ul>	<ul><li>Just getting by</li><li>Balance Cash Flow</li></ul>	Reduce your spending as you aim to spend less than what you earn.
Below Your Means	<ul><li>You spend less than what you earn.</li><li>Your expenditures are less than your income.</li></ul>	<ul><li>Free from bondage of debts</li><li>Steady cash flow</li><li>Increase savings for the raining days</li></ul>	Maintain this achievement

When you spend above your means the solution sometimes may not be having more money. All you may require is to have only what you can afford. Bible says, It is not fitting for a fool to live in luxury " – Proverbs 19:10. Most importantly, you need God's wisdom to be a good manager of money and resources. As it is written in Proverbs 17:6 "Of what use is money in the hand of a fool, since he has no desire to get wisdom? "

You must realise that God gives resources (including your money) to you to administer. Everything that exists is from God and you are to administer it from His hand. He is the fountainhead of all life and power; man is the appointed heir for its management. God has delegated the stewardship of the Earth and all in it including money to humankind, of which you are one and you are expected to bring profit from the stewardship.

One thing that is guaranteed is that, if you are a good steward of money you will always have more. If you prove yourself to be a good manager, He would not mind in entrusting more into your care. In the parable of the talents in the Bible, the Master was so delighted in how a good steward managed the five talents that was given to him that he said; ... Well-done, good and faithful servant! You have been faithful with few things; I will put you in charge of many things. Come and share our master's happiness! " (Mathew 25:21).

This shows that your profitability and prosperity make God joyful. However, for a wasteful and unprofitable steward of money will tend to poverty. Just like another story that was told in the Bible about a wasteful steward who mismanaged the resources that were committed into his hands. He was relieved of his post. In the story, there was a certain rich man who had a steward, and an accusation was brought to him that this man was wasting his goods. So he called him and said to him, 'what is this I hear about you? Give an account of your stewardship, for you can no longer be steward " (Luke 16:1-2).

Good Work Ethic

Whatever figure you multiply with zero will return zero. If you must avoid debt and you want to live in financial freedom you must be ready to work.

"He who has a slack hand becomes poor, but the hand of the diligent makes rich " - Proverbs 10:4.

If you love sleep, you will end in poverty. Keep your eyes open, and there will be plenty to eat! " (Proverbs 20:13).

The quote from the book of Mathew in the previous page, comes from an interesting story about three servants. In this story, a man called his three servants and handed over to each of them some money as starting capital for business. His expectation was for each of them to invest the money and make profit. Having known their individual ability, the starting capital was given in accordance with their capabilities.

However, it was very unfortunate that one of the three servants refused to work with his capital. While the other two industrious servants returned 100% profit on their investments, the third one returned 0% profit because he did not work with his hands. When the master returned he called this slothful servant wicked (Mathew 25:14-30). He was not only stripped of what he had he lost it to one of the diligent servants and was punished for not having good work ethic. According to the scripture, Whoever is slack in his work is a brother to him who destroys" (Proverbs 18:9).

You should not be like this unprofitable steward who can be regarded as a sluggard. As Bible put it, *"How long will you lie there, you sluggard? When will you get up from your sleep? A little sleep, a little slumber, a little folding of the hands to rest and poverty will come on you like a bandit and scarcity like an armed man "* (Proverbs 6: 9-11).

Rule Seven

Learn To

Give

"*There is one who scatters, yet increases more; and there is one who withholds more than is right, but it leads to poverty. The generous soul will be made rich, and he who waters will also be watered himself. The people will curse him who withholds grain, But blessing will be on the head of him who sells it*"
   - *Proverbs 11:24-26*

"No one has ever become poor from giving"
- The Diary of Anne Frank (1952)

I met a lady some years ago who told me that she likes seeing her collections of clothes and shoes that she has not worn in the last 5 years. She mentioned that seeing them brings delight to her. I advised her that she would derive greater joy in seeing those who are in need of these clothes and shoes wearing them than allowing them to gather dust and spider webs in her wardrobe.

Just like this lady I mentioned, there may be some clothes in your wardrobe that you have not worn in the last two years and you do not have any use for them. While these are gathering dust in your house a neighbour of yours in another community has to wait for his only shirt to dry after wash before he can go out.

I must say that when giving out your used clothes and shoes you should not give out those that are no longer usable. Remember that the purpose of giving these out is for others to use them. I read a story of a missionary who came to a church service in the city with tattered clothes. At the end of the meeting the pastor of the church asked the man why he wore tattered clothes and the man replied that, it was from the clothes sent to the mission field by the same church.

When you give to charity, you feel sense of fulfilment. In my family, we support three different charities with financial commitment every month. We always feel happy each time we receive reports from these organisations knowing fully well that we are part of their achievements and success no matter how little our contribution may be.

I notice that one of the reasons why people find it difficult to give is the fear of not having enough if they give what they have away. However, if you give, you are expressing your trust in God to provide for your own needs. The scripture says:" Cast your bread upon the waters, for you will find it after many days. Give a serving to seven and also to eight, for you
do not know what evil will be on the earth" (Ecclesiastes 11:1).

To the understanding of an ordinary mind, casting your bread upon the waters may appear wasteful. However, when you give to others; returns may not come immediately but one thing is sure, the return will come. Giving has a way of making you to have more. The Bible put it this way: "Give, and it will be given to you; a good measure – pressed down, shaken together, and running over-will be poured into your lap. For with the measure you use, it will be measure
back to you " (Luke 6:38).

I have seen this happening in my family when we give to others especially when we give to those that we know that they are not in position to give us back. The fear of depletion in our resources when we give is not real. According to Anne Frank: "No one has ever become poor from giving."

God's blessing on you is to make you a channel of blessing to others. He said: And I will make you a great nation, and I will bless you, and make your name great; and so you shall be a blessing; and I will bless those who bless you, and the one who curses you I will curse.

And in you all the families of the earth will be blessed " (Genesis 12:2-3).

You must see giving as an opportunity to go into partnership with God. When you do this, you will have fulfilment as no one ever go into partnership with God and regret it because God will never disappoint.

Giving is sowing. When you sow you should expect to reap as every farmer who sows expect harvest at the end of the season.

Two Copper Coins

I know that there is no one who does not have something to give the only difference is the level of our given or what we have to give. There is a lesson to be learnt from the story of the widow's mite. In this story, a widow gave two small coins, which were said to be her entire livelihood that she had. It is not the amount you give that matters, but the spirit and the motive by which the giving was done. The two mites given by the widow were enough to get her noticed and commended by the chief giver Himself – Our Lord Jesus Christ.

Lunch Pack

The story of a generous boy always touches me each time I read it in the Bible. This young fellow offered his lunch to Jesus not having any idea what He is going to do with it. Through this little boy's benevolence, over 5,000 men were fed plus all the women and children there. I cannot imagine how this boy would be beaming with smiles knowing that his supply was a seed that was blessed and through which many were fed and there were left overs. I am very sure that this boy will have the promise of God according the bible, which says, Feed the hungry, and help those in trouble. Then your light will shine out from the darkness, and the darkness around you will be as bright as noon. The Lord will guide you continually, giving you water when you are dry and restoring your strength. You will be like a well-watered garden, like an ever-flowing spring - Isaiah 58:10-11.

There are opportunities that abound around us to give to others if only we can be sensitive enough. Why don't you offer your lunch for one day in the week to the homeless and hungry people around you? The word of God says whoever gives to the poor lends to his maker.

Last Dinner

There was this story of a woman in the bible who gave supposedly her last dinner to a stranger. For doing this, instead of her to eating her last dinner and dying of hunger with her child she had abundance. Scriptures put it this way: " S*o he went to Zarephath. As he arrived at the gates of the village, he saw a widow gathering sticks, and he asked her, "Would you please bring me a little water in a cup?" As she was going to get it, he called to her, "Bring me a bite of bread, too." But she said, "I swear by the Lord your God that I don't have a single piece of bread in the house. And I have only a handful of flour left in the jar and a little cooking oil in the bottom of the jug. I was just gathering a few sticks to cook this last meal,* *and then my son and I will die." But Elijah said to her, "Don't be afraid! Go ahead and do just what you've said, but make a little bread for me first. Then use what's left to prepare a meal for yourself and your son. For this is what the Lord, the God of Israel, says: There will always be flour and olive oil left in your containers until the time when the Lord sends rain and the crops grow again!" So she did as Elijah said, and she and Elijah and her family continued to eat for many days. There was always enough flour and olive oil left in the containers, just as the Lord had promised through Elijah - 1Kings 17:10-16 NLT.*

God promises that those who give generously will receive back more than they gave. This may be contrary to natural man's law, which is always to get as much as you can and sometimes even get from those who do not have as much as you do. God blesses those who are kind and generous with their money and materials. Bible says "One person gives freely, yet gains more; another withholds what is right, only to become poor. A generous person will be enriched, and the one who gives a drink of water will receive water. People will curse anyone who hoards grain, but a blessing will come to the one who sells it" (Proverbs 11:24-26).

Chocolate Box

Have you ever considered how children behave when you ask them to give you a piece out of the bundle of what you have just given them? Let us illustrate it this way with the story of Johnson who bought a pack of chocolate on his way from work for his son Jack who is four years old.

Johnson: Jack! Johnson called his son.

Jack: Yes! Daddy you're welcome.

Johnson: He handed over the pack of chocolate to Jack.

Jack: He opened it and thanked his dad for the pack of chocolate and starts to eat. Thank you, dad, he said.

Johnson: As Jack opened the box to start eating, his father Jackson asked Jack for a piece out of it. Jack can I have a piece of chocolate?

Jack: He refused and begins to cry as Johnson attempted to take one piece from the box.

Do you know why Jack refused? He refused because he was ignorant of the source of the chocolate, because if he has understanding that his father who gave the whole box to him can afford more boxes of chocolate; he would have obliged his father.

For those who are Christians, this is how some behave when it comes to giving their tithes. Tithes does not necessarily have to be cash, it is the tenth part of any thing that is released and consecrated and set apart for God. Out of what God has given us He only requires us to give one tenth of it and most of us don't want to give back or give reluctantly. We should understand that God is the giver of all things and He is able to do exceedingly abundantly above all we ask or think according to the power that works in us.

If our giving is withheld, we are robbing God of the privilege of pouring out great and overflowing blessings on us. You could imagine how delightful it would have been for Johnson if his son Jack had willingly given him a piece of the chocolate from the box.

When you give your tithes and offerings, not only that God will pour His blessing on you He will also protect them as He said
"I will prevent pests from devouring your crops, and the vines in your fields will not drop their fruit before it is ripe" (Malachi 3:11)

It is a great privilege to be a giver.

Appendix

Yourbudgetsheet

Your Name:

YourIncome

Earnings	Amount	Frequency
Client's salary or wages (take home)	£	
Partner's salary or wages (take home)	£	
Other earnings (including self employment)	£	

Benefitsandtaxcredits	Amount	Frequency
Universal Credit	£	
Jobseeker's Allowance (Income-based)	£	
Jobseeker's Allowance (Contribution-based)	£	
Income Support	£	
Working Tax Credit	£	
Child Tax Credit	£	
Child Benefit	£	
Employment & Support Allowance / Statutory Sick Pay	£	
Disability benefits	£	
Carer's Allowance	£	
Local Housing Allowance / Housing Benefit	£	
Council Tax support	£	
Other benefits/tax credits (e.g. maternity benefits)	£	

Pensions	Amount	Frequency
State pension(s)	£	
Private or work pension(s)	£	
Pension Credit	£	
Other pensions	£	

Otherincome	Amount	Frequency
Maintenance or child support	£	
Boarders or Lodgers	£	
Non-dependant contributions	£	
Student loans and grants	£	
Other income	£	

Homeandcontents	Amount	Frequency
Rent	£	
Ground rent & service charges (factor fees if you live in Scotland)	£	
Mortgage	£	
Mortgage endowment	£	
Secured loans	£	
Council tax/rates (including water charge if you live in Scotland and rates in NI)	£	
Appliance & furniture rental (including appliance and furniture HP, conditional sale and so on)	£	
TV licence	£	
Other costs	£	

Utilities	Amount	Frequency
Electricity	£	
Gas	£	
Other costs (including coal, oil, calor gas etc.)	£	
Other expenditure	£	

Water	Amount	Frequency
Water supply	£	
Water waste	£	

Careandhealthcosts	Amount	Frequency
Childcare costs	£	
Adult care costs	£	
Child maintenance or child support	£	
Prescriptions and medicines	£	
Dentistry and opticians	£	
Other health costs	£	

Transportandtravel	Amount	Frequency
Public transport (work, school, shopping etc)	£	
Hire Purchase or conditional sale vehicle	£	
Car insurance	£	
Road tax	£	
MOT and ongoing maintenance	£	
Breakdown cover	£	
Fuel, parking and toll road charges	£	
Other (e.g. taxis)	£	

School costs	Amount	Frequency
School Uniform	£	
After-school clubs and school trips	£	
Other school costs	£	

Pensions and insurances	Amount	Frequency
Pension payments	£	
Life insurance	£	
Mortgage payment protection insurance	£	
Building and contents insurance	£	
Health insurance (medical or accident or dental)	£	
Other pension costs	£	

Professional costs	Amount	Frequency
Professional courses	£	
Union fees	£	
Professional fees	£	
Other professional costs	£	

Other essential costs	Amount	Frequency
Other essential costs	£	

Communications and leisure	Amount	Frequency
Home phone, internet, TV package (including film subscriptions)	£	
Mobile phone	£	
Hobbies, leisure or sport (e.g. socialising, eating out, outings, clubs, leisure courses)	£	
Gifts (e.g. birthdays, festivals, charity donations)	£	
Pocket money	£	
Newspapers and magazines	£	
Other leisure costs	£	

Food and housekeeping	Amount	Frequency
Groceries (e.g. food, pet food, non-alcoholic drinks, cleaning)	£	
Nappies and baby items	£	
School meals and meals at work	£	
Laundry and dry cleaning	£	
Alcohol	£	
Smoking products	£	
Vet bills and pet insurance	£	
House repairs and maintenance	£	
Other food and housekeeping costs	£	

Personal Costs

	Amount	Frequency
Clothing and footwear	£	
Hairdressing	£	
Toiletries	£	
Other personal costs	£	

Savings	Amount	Frequency
Monthly saving amount	£	

Your debts

List the details of your debts (if any)

Type of debt	Amount owed	Creditor	Reference
	£		
	£		
	£		
	£		
	£		
	£		
	£		
	£		
	£		
	£		
	£		
	£		

This small book is the result of my own experiences over nine years in money advice. These self-acclaimed rules are tried and tested techniques and my intention is to make Money handling process simple by showing how these 'rules' can be applied practically to real life situations. The aim of writing this book is to show you how to avoid pitfalls that may arise in money handling.

I have briefly discussed seven cardinal rules which in my opinion are a 'sine qua non' for anyone who wants to enjoy a financial freedom within their available resources. I believe if these rules are applied proactively to your day to day use and management of your money it will be of great assistance in the future. Whatever effort you put in place in organising your finances to yield good result now and in the future. – Femi Adedayo

"From his considerable experience as a money adviser and his deep Christian faith Femi Adedayo in his second book is able to share great wisdom based on real experience in the management of money distilled into his Seven Cardinal Rules of Debt Avoidance." – David B. Gloin

"I like the pattern of the writing of this book, it's illustrative and factually enlightening its audience" – David Akinwusi

Femi Adedayo
femiadedayo@yahoo.com

Seven Cardinal Rules Of Debt Avoidance

PUBLICATION 2016
www.globalreachmedia.co.uk info@globalreachmedia.co.uk
+447900223577

London, United Kingdom